The New Toe
poems to tickle your funnybone
by Jeannie McGregor with Illustrations by Bill Brownridge

Bayeux Arts Inc.

Copyright © Jeannie McGregor and Bill Brownridge
All rights reserved

Bayeux Arts Inc.
119 Stratton Crescent S.W.
Calgary, Alberta, Canada T3H 1T7

Canadian Catalogue in Publication Data

McGegor, Jeannie
  The New Toe: Poems to tickle your funnybone

  ISBN 1-896209-60-2
  1. Children's poetry, Canadian (English)* 2. Humorous poetry, Canadian (English)* I. Brownridge, Bill. II. Title.
  PS8575.G82P63 2001   jC811'.6   C2001-910103-1
  PZ7.M169952Po 2001

Printed in Hong Kong

The publisher gratefully acknowledges the generous support of the Canada Council for the Arts, the Alberta Foundation for the Arts, and the Government of Canada through the Book Publishing Industry Development Program.

Dedication
In loving memory of my parents,
Eileen and Mac McGregor

Acknowledgements
This book was the vision of Kate Goldsmith,
who showed my poetry to Bill Brownridge
in the Summer of 1998, in hopes
that a book would result.
Both Bill and I thank her for
bringing us together.

Special thanks go to Laurel McIndoe and
Filma Hewitt for their editorial assistance.

Jeannie McGregor

Contents

The New Toe	8
Wings	10
Poor Sammy!	13
That Word	14
If Centipedes Wore Running Shoes	16
Little Secrets	18
Green	20
Pigs	22
The Bubble	25

The Dream	26
The Cowlick	28
Clancy Dugan	30
The Witch	32
The Ref	34
Buzzzz	37
No Lie	39
The Christmas Concert	40
The Martian	44

The New Toe

Last night, while getting ready for bed,
I took off my socks
and noticed a new toe.
I said, "Holy Cow!
You just never know!"

I showed my mom
who'd been feeding the cat.
"Look — a new toe."
She said, "Oh my word!
You just never know!"

I next showed my dad
who'd been reading a book.
"Look — a new toe."
He said, "Holy jumpers!
You just never know!"

I then showed my brother
who's never impressed.
"Look — a new toe."
He just rolled his eyes
and he said, "Yeah — so?"

Wings

My brother made some cardboard wings
and here's the reason why.
It seems the boy's ambition
is to soar right through the sky.

He's jumping from the fence once more,
wings flapping with great might.
I guess he thinks, eventually,
that he will get it right.

I really ought to tell him
that his war cannot be won,
but watching as he flaps those wings
is sure a lot of fun.

So I will sit and watch him try
and not tell him the truth —
unless, of course, his plan becomes
to fly right off the roof.

Poor Sammy!

My turtle died just yesterday,
which really made me cry.
I could not understand why God
would make my turtle die.

My mom told me poor Sammy
would be happier in Heaven
and so we held a funeral
around the hour of seven.

Three kids arrived with flowers
and that sure did make me glad.
It all was so exciting
that I wasn't quite so sad.

We placed Sam in a jewelry box,
surrounded by some cotton.
We sang a hymn and said that Sam
would never be forgotten.

We dug a hole six inches deep
and put the box inside,
replaced the dirt, and sang again,
then everybody cried.

Now today my folks are trying
to really cheer me up.
The time is right, I do believe,
to ask them for a pup.

That Word

Our parrot, Polly, says a word
I'm not allowed to say,
and when she does, it's plain to see,
it ruins my parents' day.

When Polly says that nasty word,
it causes Mom to shriek,
"You really are a nasty bird!
I ought to glue your beak!"

When Polly says that filthy word,
in front of dear, old Dad,
his face will turn the darkest red
because he's boiling mad.

My parents say that Polly got
that word from our t.v.
What they don't know is that she
learned that dirty word from me!

If Centipedes Wore Running Shoes

If centipedes wore running shoes,
their lives would sure be rough,
'cause keeping all the laces tied,
I'm sure would be quite tough.

They'd have to get up early
just to get their footwear on,
and by the time they finished,
why, the morning would be gone.

They'd be afraid to visit friends
for what might be in store,
is expectations that they take
their shoes off at the door.

Nonetheless, the thought that really
makes me think — my gosh!
is when I think of all the socks
those centipedes would wash.

Little Secrets

God knows my little secrets,
my mother told me so.
She said my Maker watches me,
wherever I may go.

He knows when I am trying
to do my very best.
He knows if all the food I eat
has properly been blessed.

He watches as I climb up,
upon a kitchen chair,
and when I sneak more cookies,
I know I feel his stare.

But it doesn't seem to matter
if I'm a little bad,
'cause so far he's not bothered
to tell my mom and dad.

Green

Ashley is the strangest kid
that you have ever seen.
The reason is the girl's obsession
with the colour green.

Her socks and shoes and all her clothes
are green as green can be.
When looking at her books and pens,
yes, green is all you see.

Her pillows, sheets, her bedspread too,
her rug, her desk, her blind,
they are the greenest, greeny green
that you will ever find.

It makes me nervous all this green!
It worries me at night!
For I am Ashley's little dog,
and so far, I'm still white.

Pigs

When Heaven first created pigs,
it must have caused a stir,
for clearly since they're bare and pink,
someone forgot the fur.

The tail is odd and useless too,
a fact you can't deny.
It's just a little, curled-up thing,
that couldn't swat a fly.

The snout, of course, is really dumb,
for when the wind does gust,
with nostrils open to the world,
the pig fills up with dust.

Yes, looking at the pig, I must admit,
I get a laugh!
I am so thankful God decreed that
I'd be the giraffe.

The Bubble

Alice liked to chew some gum;
she'd chew it all day through,
and then one day, the poor, dear girl
a great, big bubble blew.

No sooner was the bubble blown,
she lifted from the ground.
She sailed above the roofs and trees;
the girl was Heaven-bound.

She could have popped that bubble
when she first began to fly,
and had she done the clever thing,
she'd not be in the sky.

Her choice was not because she was
a girl who liked a dare.
In truth, she feared she'd pop the thing
and she'd have sticky hair.

And so today she floats around;
the girl is in distress,
for with the wind and rain and such,
her hair's an awful mess!

The Dream

Last night after
root beer and potato chips,
I dreamed
a big dog
with big teeth
chased me.

I didn't know why
he was mad at me.
I like dogs.
Dogs like me,
except this one.

I raced down an alley.
He raced after me.
I jumped a small hedge.
He jumped after me.

Then I did
the most amazing thing.
I ran straight up a tree
and realized
I was a cat.

The Cowlick

I have a cowlick in my hair
that drives me quite insane.
Those strands of hair will not lie down;
it's hair you cannot train.

Yet Tuesday morning when I woke,
I had a different thought —
I'd make those hairs behave for once,
no matter how they fought.

I combed and brushed and combed some more,
but still they would not lie,
and so I got my brother's gel —
it sure was worth a try!

I took a great, big glob of gel
and slapped it on that hair,
so when the cowlick popped back up,
all I could do was stare!

Five bobby pins would not keep down
those nasty, stubborn strands,
and neither would, you won't believe,
my sister's three hairbands.

I now agree I lost my cool!
Indeed, I went too far!
I used a tube of Superglu
before I used the tar.

Despite all that, those hairs soon poked
out from that tar so black,
yet I would not admit defeat,
and made one last attack.

"You'll stand no longer, stupid hair!"
I ranted and I raved,
but now I'm truly sorry 'bout
the bald spot that I shaved.

Clancy Dugan

Clancy Dugan's in my class;
he's really quite the guy,
and 'cause of all the things he does,
he makes the hours fly.

When the class is reading books
and all the room is quiet,
that's when Clancy Dugan
will be sure to start a riot.

His eyes will drift to Katie Lukes
and from his desk he'll take,
a present for that high-strung girl,
a rubber rattle snake.

While Katie's lost inside her book,
sly Clancy takes his aim,
and Clancy's sure to end up in
The Snake Toss Hall of Fame.

'Cause when that rubber rattler
just goes sailing through the air,
it always lands on Katie's book,
beneath the poor girl's stare.

The next part is my favorite
because Katie screams so loud,
and teachers run from everywhere,
and soon, there's quite a crowd.

Miss Evans then takes Clancy down
to see old Mr. Black,
who only yells and shouts a lot,
then Clancy comes right back.

Yes, this year I am learning lots!
I really love grade four,
but if it weren't for Clancy,
I know it would be a bore!

The Witch

One night some lightning cracked the sky
and lit up my whole room,
and from my window I then spied
an old witch on a broom.

That hag was flying past the moon
like in a picture book.
I was so scared when I saw her,
I will admit, I shook.

Then she saw me and swooped right down
along that star-filled road.
She waved her wand, said magic words,
and now I am a toad!

Therefore, my friend, when lightning streaks,
and thunder roars, "Come see!"
You just might spot an evil witch,
who makes you look like me.

The Ref

This hockey game's a nightmare,
and the ref's the reason why.
There's no way in a million years
I'll understand that guy.

He sees things happen on the ice
that no one else can see,
and I'm convinced this certain ref's
obsessed with watching me!

The penalty box is now my home
and I'm just boiling mad.
The thing that bugs me most of all
is that the ref's my dad!

Buzzzz

A fly came buzzing round my head,
the filthy little beast!
And so I grabbed the swatter;
it soon would be deceased.

It settled on a lampshade —
I crept up to that bug,
and after a most mighty swing,
the lamp crashed to the rug.

I soon heard that same buzzing,
and quickly, I saw why,
for settled on Mom's china bowl
was that same rotten fly.

I'm sure I heard it laughing,
and taunting, "Can't catch me!"
And so my mother's china bowl
was smashed for all to see.

When Mom saw, she went crazy,
and I was forced to lie,
that Tom, our cat, just lost his mind
while chasing some darn fly.

At first, she bought my story.
T'was going just as planned,
until my mother noticed what
I still held in my hand.

No Lie

My brother always doubts me,
no matter what I say.
His favorite words are "Prove it",
or maybe just, "No way".

But now he's where I want him,
outside — STUCK in the cold.
He's lots of time to realize
it was no lie I told.

I see snow now begin to fall;
the flakes are big and white.
I think about that kid out there
but know he'll be all right.

He'll soon be found I'm certain,
although he sure can't yell,
and I'll get heck for leaving him
'cause Mom and Dad he'll tell.

I'll tell my folks I warned him,
t'was something not to try.
I'll tell them that he told me
he thought it was a lie.

They'll send me to my bedroom,
to think about my sin,
but when I think about the scene,
all I can do is grin.

Tomorrow I will tell my friends;
tomorrow I will boast,
of how I got that stupid kid
to lick that metal post!

The Christmas Concert

The Christmas concert sure was fun
though Miss Blake's still upset.
Because so many things went wrong,
she's not recovered yet.

The truth is Clarence is a pain
so got what he deserved,
and since that evening, Clarence
has been thoroughly unnerved.

Clarence Henry was the star
of Miss Blake's Christmas play.
She said his acting was "Superb!"
on each rehearsal day.

Yes, Clarence Henry really thought
that he was just so great,
for little did Miss Blake or he
know what would be his fate.

The concert was a big event
and everybody came.
Clarence Henry told us all
his role would bring him fame.

The play would start at eight o'clock;
the hour did arrive,
and still today, I wonder how
old Clarence did survive.

In the center of the stage
he stood and all was still.
The sight of all those happy folks
sure seemed to make him ill.

Clarence Henry smiled a bit
and then his eyes just rolled,
and then in front of everyone,
poor Clarence seemed to fold.

He fell into the Christmas tree
which fell on top of Meg,
who started screaming frantically,
"I think it broke my leg!"

A bunch of girls began to scream,
and some girls even cried.
Because poor Clarence lay so still,
they thought that he had died.

Backstage there was a billy goat
we'd borrowed for the play.
The beast was tied securely
and just munching on some hay.

While the girls were screaming
and poor Clarence lay onstage,
suddenly, that goat was freed
which started his rampage.

They want to know who freed that goat
which was the final straw
in ending that fiasco,
yet I'm certain — NO ONE SAW!

Eventually, it all worked out
and Clarence sure was right.
Just like our star predicted —
he's been famous since that night!

The Martian

My brother is an alien;
he told me so today.
He said he's from the planet Mars
but on the earth to stay.

His job is just to look and act
like any normal child,
but each month for the Martian world,
his spy report is filed.

He said when no one is around,
he eats worms one by one,
because to Martians worms taste good
and eating them is fun.

He said his real skin is bright green!
He said he has three eyes!
He said he has four bat-like wings!
He told me that he flies!

I asked him questions by the score,
about his life on Mars.
He told me things about deep space
and all about the stars.

I talked for hours in my room
with this Martian sleuth,
'cause I had fun pretending that
I thought he spoke the truth.